Safety First!

Safety at Home

by Lucia Raatma

Consultant:
Anara Guard, MLS
Research Associate
Children's Safety Network

Bridgestone Books
an imprint of Capstone Press
Mankato, Minnesota

Bridgestone Books are published by Capstone Press
151 Good Counsel Drive, P.O. Box 669, Mankato, Minnesota 56002
http://www.capstone-press.com

Library of Congress Cataloging-in-Publication Data
Raatma, Lucia.
Safety at Home/by Lucia Raatma.
    p. cm.—(Safety first)
Includes bibliographical references (p. 24) and index.
Summary: Explains how to prevent accidents around the home and deal with
emergencies, covering such topics as electricity, medicines, and fires.
ISBN 0-7368-0061-1
1. Home accidents—Prevention—Juvenile literature. 2. Safety education—Juvenile
literature. [1. Safety.] I. Title. II. Series: Raatma, Lucia. Safety first.
HV675.5.R3 1999
613.6—DC21
                                                                                    98-18425
                                                                                         CIP
                                                                                          AC

Editorial Credits
Rebecca Glaser, editor; Clay Schotzko/Icon Productions, cover designer;
  Sheri Gosewisch, photo researcher

Photo Credits
Barb Stitzer, cover, 4, 6, 8, 10, 12, 14, 16, 18, 20

2 3 4 5 6 06 05 04 03 02

Table of Contents

Safe Homes

Homes should be safe. But accidents may happen in homes. You can learn how to keep some accidents from happening. You can also learn what to do if accidents happen. You can make your home safe.

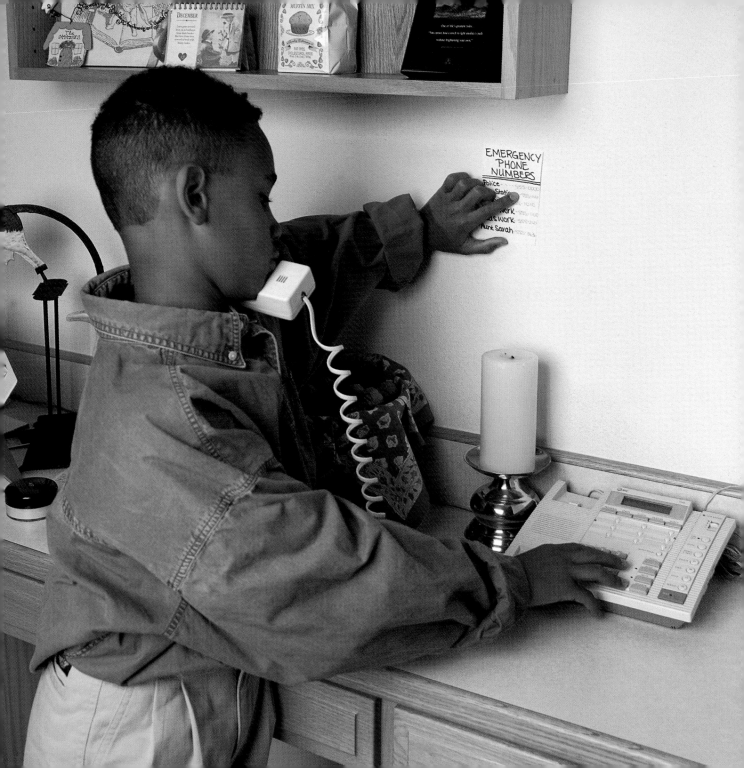

Emergencies

An emergency is a sudden danger like a fire. Talk with a parent or another adult about emergencies. Find out what you should do if accidents happen. Know who to call in an emergency.

Fire Safety

Fires can destroy homes and hurt people. Never play with matches or lighters. You could start fires. An adult should check the smoke detectors in your home. Smoke detectors warn people of smoke. Learn how to leave your home in case a fire starts. Plan escape routes with your family.

Safety on Stairs

Accidents can happen on stairs. Do not leave things like toys or shoes on stairs. Someone could trip and fall. Do not run on stairs. Hold the hand rail when going up and down stairs. Do not sit or slide on the hand rail. You could get hurt.

Safety around Doors and Windows

Accidents can happen around doors and windows. Close doors slowly and carefully. Do not lean out of windows or push on screens. You could fall out and hurt yourself. Climb out of windows only in emergencies.

Safety in the Kitchen

Adults should always help children in the kitchen. You should stay away from the stove and oven. You could get burned. Ask an adult to help you cut food. You could cut yourself with sharp knives.

Safety in the Bathroom

Be careful around water in the bathroom. Wipe up any water on the floor. People could slip and fall on wet floors. Be careful when turning on the water. Water that is too hot can burn your skin.

Safety around Medicines

Medicines are drugs people take when they are sick. They make people feel better. But the wrong kind of medicine could make you sick. Do not take any medicines unless an adult says you can. The adult should tell you how much to take.

Safety around Electricity

Electricity is power. People plug things like TVs into outlets for electricity. But electricity can hurt you. Ask an adult to plug in things for you. Ask an adult to cover outlets that are not in use.

Hands on: Make a Phone List

You need to know who to call during emergencies. Ask a parent or other adult to help you. You can make a list of phone numbers. Keep your list by the phone.

<u>What You Need</u>

A parent or other adult to help   A phone book
Paper   Markers

<u>What You Do</u>

1. First, write your own address and phone number. You may need to tell them to someone during an emergency.
2. Ask a parent to help you find important phone numbers. Write the name and number of each place. Include numbers for the police and fire departments. Include the number for the hospital.
3. Draw a picture by each number. For example, draw fire next to the fire department phone number. The pictures can help you find the numbers easily.
4. Write your parents' work phone numbers.
5. Ask your parents who else you can call in emergencies. Write these names and numbers also.
6. Make a list to hang by each phone in your home.

Words to Know

accident (AK-si-duhnt)—when a person is hurt; an accident is not expected.

electricity (i-lek-TRISS-uh-tee)—power

emergency (i-MUHR-juhn-see)—a sudden danger like a fire or crash

escape route (ess-KAPE ROUT)—a way to leave a building in an emergency

outlet (OUT-let)—a place where people plug in things for electricity

Read More

Children's Hospital at Yale-New Haven. *Now I Know Better: Kids Tell Kids about Safety.* Brookfield, Conn.: Millbrook Press, 1996.

Gutman, Bill. *Hazards at Home.* New York: Twenty-First Century Books, 1996.

Loewen, Nancy. *Home Safety.* Plymouth, Minn.: Child's World, 1997.

Internet Sites

Children Home Alone
http://www.cfc-efc.ca/docs/unknown/tied2/00000724.htm
Home Fire Safety
http://www.ou.edu/oupd/fireprev.htm
Stay Alert, Stay Safe
http://www.sass.ca/kmenu.htm

Index